Kennedy

by James Gracie

Lang**Syne**

PUBLISHING

WRITING *to* REMEMBER

LangSyne

PUBLISHING

WRITING *to* REMEMBER

79 Main Street, Newtongrange,
Midlothian EH22 4NA
Tel: 0131 344 0414   Fax: 0845 075 6085
E-mail: info@lang-syne.co.uk
www.langsyneshop.co.uk

Design by Dorothy Meikle
Printed by Ricoh Print Scotland
© Lang Syne Publishers Ltd 2015

ISBN 978-1-85217-050-9

Kennedy

SEPT NAMES INCLUDE:

Carrick
Cassels
Cassillis
MacWalrick

Kennedy

MOTTO:
Consider the end

CREST:
A swimming dolphin

TERRITORY:
Carrick and Galloway

Chapter one:

The origins of the clan system

by Rennie McOwan

The original Scottish clans of the Highlands and the great families of the Lowlands and Borders were gatherings of families, relatives, allies and neighbours for mutual protection against rivals or invaders.

Scotland experienced invasion from the Vikings, the Romans and English armies from the south. The Norman invasion of what is now England also had an influence on land-holding in Scotland. Some of these invaders stayed on and in time became 'Scottish'.

The word clan derives from the Gaelic language term 'clann', meaning children, and it was first used many centuries ago as communities were formed around tribal lands in glens and mountain fastnesses.

The format of clans changed over the centuries, but at its best the chief and his family held the land on behalf of all, like trustees, and the ordinary clansmen and women believed they had a blood relationship with the founder of their clan.

There were two way duties and obligations. An inadequate chief could be deposed and replaced by someone of greater ability.

Clan people had an immense pride in race. Their relationship with the chief was like adult children to a father and they had a real dignity.

The concept of clanship is very old and a more feudal notion of authority gradually crept in.

Pictland, for instance, was divided into seven principalities ruled by feudal leaders who were the strongest and most charismatic leaders of their particular groups.

By the sixth century the 'British' kingdoms of Strathclyde, Lothian and Celtic Dalriada (Argyll) had emerged and Scotland, as one nation, began to take shape in the time of King Kenneth MacAlpin.

Some chiefs claimed descent from

ancient kings which may not have been accurate in every case.

By the twelfth and thirteenth centuries the clans and families were more strongly brought under the central control of Scottish monarchs.

Lands were awarded and administered more and more under royal favour, yet the power of the area clan chiefs was still very great.

The long wars to ensure Scotland's independence against the expansionist ideas of English monarchs extended the influence of some clans and reduced the lands of others.

Those who supported Scotland's greatest king, Robert the Bruce, were awarded the territories of the families who had opposed his claim to the Scottish throne.

In the Scottish Borders country – the notorious Debatable Lands – the great families built up a ferocious reputation for providing warlike men accustomed to raiding into England and occasionally fighting one another.

Chiefs had the power to dispense justice and to confiscate lands and clan warfare produced a society where martial virtues – courage, hardiness, tenacity – were greatly admired.

Gradually the relationship between the clans and the Crown became strained as Scottish monarchs became more orientated to life in the Lowlands and, on occasion, towards England.

The Highland clans spoke a different language, Gaelic, whereas the language of Lowland Scotland and the court was Scots and in more modern times, English.

Highlanders dressed differently, had different customs, and their wild mountain land sometimes seemed almost foreign to people living in the Lowlands.

It must be emphasised that Gaelic culture was very rich and story-telling, poetry, piping, the clarsach (harp) and other music all flourished and were greatly respected.

Highland culture was different from other parts of Scotland but it was not inferior or less sophisticated.

Central Government, whether in London or Edinburgh, sometimes saw the Gaelic clans as

"The spirit of the clan means much to thousands of people"

a challenge to their authority and some sent expeditions into the Highlands and west to crush the power of the Lords of the Isles.

Nevertheless, when the eighteenth century Jacobite Risings came along the cause of the Stuarts was mainly supported by Highland clans.

The word Jacobite comes from the Latin for James – Jacobus. The Jacobites wanted to restore the exiled Stuarts to the throne of Britain.

The monarchies of Scotland and England became one in 1603 when King James VI of Scotland (1st of England) gained the English throne after Queen Elizabeth died.

The Union of Parliaments of Scotland and England, the Treaty of Union, took place in 1707.

Some Highland clans, of course, and Lowland families opposed the Jacobites and supported the incoming Hanoverians.

After the Jacobite cause finally went down at Culloden in 1746 a kind of ethnic cleansing took place. The power of the chiefs was curtailed. Tartan and the pipes were banned in law.

Many emigrated, some because they

wanted to, some because they were evicted by force. In addition, many Highlanders left for the cities of the south to seek work.

Many of the clan lands became home to sheep and deer shooting estates.

But the warlike traditions of the clans and the great Lowland and Border families lived on, with their descendants fighting bravely for freedom in two world wars.

Remember the men from whence you came, says the Gaelic proverb, and to that could be added the role of many heroic women.

The spirit of the clan, of having roots, whether Highland or Lowland, means much to thousands of people.

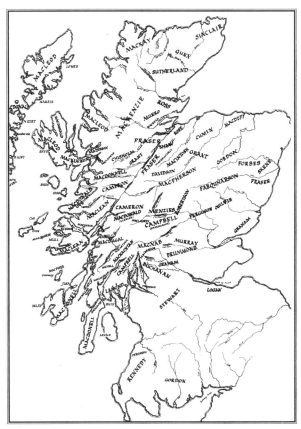

A map of the clans' homelands

Chapter two:

Men of mystery

The Kennedys (Gaelic Ceannaideach) are one of the great Lowland families of Scotland, their heartland being that southern portion of Ayrshire called Carrick.

Some claim that they crossed from Ireland and settled in south west Scotland. Their progenitor was on Céndetig ("ugly-headed") who is mentioned in the book of Leinster.

Others say they are descended from one Cunedda, a minor prince of the Votadini, a British tribe whose capital was either Edinburgh or Traprain Law.

In the "Black Book of Scone" (now lost) it was claimed that they came from the Western Isles, and that the name was originally Mackenane or Mackenede, both meaning "son of Kenneth".

One of these "sons of Kenneth", living during the reign of Malcolm II (105-1053) was the founder of the clan.

His descendants were supposed to have fought alongside Alexander III (1249-1286) against the Danes at the Battle of Largs in 1263. For this, he was given the lands of Dunure in Carrick.

However, the name was actually in use in south west Scotland long before the reign of Alexander III, and it may even be that the Kennedys are descended from early lords of Galloway.

Any one of the above explanations may be the right one, and unless any new evidence is unearthed, the origins of the Kennedys will remain a mystery.

In 1158, Henry Kennedi is named as one of the rebels in a plot against Roland, earl of Galloway. And there was a Gilbert Mackenedi who witnessed a charter in the reign of William the Lion (1165-1214).

We find a Gillescop MacKenedi mentioned as Steward of Carrick in 1243, and a charter of Duncan, 1st earl of Carrick (died 1250), was witnessed by one "Murthac the Steward".

This was probably the same Murthac Mackenedi who witnessed another charter in the same year.

By about 1260, however, the name was becoming increasingly common. Murthac Mackenedy, Samuel Mackenedi and Henry Mackenedi were members of the assizes at Ayr on July 21 1260.

And on September 22, Murthac and Henry were members of another assize court this time at Girvan.

Kennedys certainly fought alongside Wallace and Bruce. But there were Kennedys on the English side as well. One Alexander Kennedy, "clerico" (suggesting that he was in holy orders) swore fealty to Edward I of England in 1296.

In the same year, he witnessed John Baliol's renunciation of the treaty with France which had established the Auld Alliance.

However, Kennedys later fought for the French against England, and we know that a group of Scottish mercenaries who were in Joan of Arc's army in the early 15th century was commanded by a Kennedy.

Before the 14th century, the name appears in various spellings, mostly with the "mac" prefix, though sometimes without.

By at least 1346, however, the prefix had been dropped completely. In the year we first hear of John Kennedy, head of the Kennedys of Dunure.

His first wife was Marjorie Montgomerie, and from her he acquired the important lands of Cassillis, near Dunure. From then on the Dunure branch became known as the Kennedys of Cassillis, and they chose to live in Cassillis Castle near Dalrymple.

Neil, 2nd earl of Carrick, had at one time granted a charter to his nephew Roland de Carrick "and his heirs" creating him kenkynol or chief of his branch of the family.

In 1372 Robert II, 1st Stewart king reaffirmed this charter in favour of that same John Kennedy of Dunure.

However, this kenkynolship, by royal charter, had to pass through the female line John's second wife was Mary de Carrick, and from her he and his heirs obtained the title. He was now chieftain, not only of the Kennedys, but of a family with direct links to the earldom of Carrick.

Today the earldom is a royal one, and borne by the heir to the throne. Prince Charles is therefore the present earl.

John's son was Sir Gilbert Kennedy (1340-1408). His son James married Princess Mary, daughter of Robert III, and from that time there was royal blood in the main Kennedy line.

Their son Gilbert was one of the Regents of Scotland during James III's minority, and in 1457 created 1st Lord Kennedy.

Another son was more famous, however. He was James, who became Bishop of St Andrews. He was one of the great statesmen of his time, and was guardian and councillor to James III.

By now, the family was beginning to fragment into minor, but still powerful, cadet branches. The Kennedys, it seems, were ambitious people, and second and third sons were not

David, third Lord Kennedy,
was killed at Flodden in 1513

content to play second fiddle. They carved out careers and powerful families for themselves.

Apart from the main Cassillis line, there were the Kennedys of Bargany, the Kennedys of Kirkmichael, the Kennedys of Girvanmains, and so on. And within each minor line there were further cadet branches.

David, 3rd Lord Kennedy, was created 1st Earl of Cassillis in 1509. However, he was killed at Flodden in 1513.

About that time, many minor Kennedy lairdships disappear from the scene, no doubt because the lairds and their retainers perished also.

The Kennedys eventually spread south into Wigtownshire and Kirkcudbrightshire. The main stronghold in the south was Castle Kennedy near Stranraer. The lands had been acquired in 1482 by John, 2nd Lord Kennedy.

The park lands were laid out as magnificent gardens by the Earl of Stair, who eventually bought them, and can now be visited.

Chapter three:

Legends and dark deeds

No history of the Kennedys would be complete without the famous story of the "roasting of the abbot" in 1570.

At the Reformation, the Abbey o Crossraguel's possessions and lands were placed in the hands of Allan Stewart, who was styled "Commendator of Crossraguel". He was strictly speaking, not an abbot, but he enjoyed the powers and privileges of one.

Gilbert, 4th Earl of Cassillis, was "an wery greidy man", and coveted the abbey lands Promises and threats had failed to make Allan sign them over, so Gilbert captured him and brought him to Dunure Castle.

There he had him tied to a spit, then basted and roasted over an open fire until he signed away the lands.

He was eventually rescued by his brother-in-law, Kennedy of Bargany, sworn enemy o

Gilbert. Allan rescinded his signature, and appealed to the Crown.

The Crown, however, thought better of crossing so powerful a man as Gilbert, and did nothing. The 4th Earl therefore kept the Crossraguel lands.

Another well-known story about the Kennedys, however, has no basis in fact. This concerns Sir John Faa of Dunbar, nicknamed 'Johnny Faa, King of the Gypsies".

It seems that Lady Jean Hamilton, daughter of the Earl of Haddington, unwillingly married John, 6th Earl of Cassillis. However, she was in love with another – Sir John Faa.

She went reluctantly to live in Ayrshire, and eventually bore the Earl many children. However, she never forgot Sir John, and he never forgot her.

Then, one day, when the Earl was in London on church business, Sir John returned to rescue Jean from Cassillis Castle. With him were fourteen gypsies, and he himself was disguised as one.

They tricked their way into the castle, and rescued Jean. However, the Earl returned early from London, and set out in pursuit. He caught up with the runaways and took them to Cassillis, where he made Jean watch as Johnny Faa and the gypsies were hanged from the Earl's "dule-tree".

Thereafter Jean was incarcerated within Maybole Castle, where she spent her days making tapestries. Above one window of the castle you can still see carvings which are said to represent Johnny and his gypsies.

The story is completely untrue, as letters written by the 6th Earl on the death of his countess show they were a close couple. The story is found in many forms throughout Europe, and has formed the basis of many a ballad.

The Kennedys were fighters. They fought with their Ayrshire neighbours, but most especially they fought among themselves.

The great Kennedy feud was between the Cassillis and Bargany branches. The reasons were complicated, and not always understood even by the families themselves.

It lasted over two generations in the 16th century, and dragged in minor Kennedys, other families in the area, and serfs who owed allegiance to either family.

They even fought on opposite sides at the Battle of Langside in 1568. Carrick was awash with blood, and the feud only ended with the death of the head of the Barganys in 1601.

The Bargany stronghold was Ardstinchar Castle at Ballantrae. The head of the Barganys, Gilbert Kennedy, and some of his men had been

Kennedy fought Kennedy at the Battle of Langside

Settling old scores

riding home from Ayr, and were met by John, 5th Earl of Cassillis and 200 men near Maybole. Knowing he was outnumbered, Gilbert tried to ride round them.

But the Cassillis men were spoiling for a fight, and one duly took place. Gilbert was wounded and died five days later in Ayr.

His widow had him buried in a magnificent tomb within Ballantrae church, and, though the church is now gone, you can still see it today in the churchyard.

The funeral procession was said to comprise over 1,000 people, with Earls and Lords among them. His nephew carried a banner which read "Judge and Revenge my Cause, O Lord!"

However, no revenge took place, and his heir Thomas died childless in 1621. With him, the Bargany line died out.

After the death of Gilbert, when the Earls of Cassillis became undisputed heads of the whole family, the Kennedys settled down to more peaceful pursuits.

Chapter four:

Of land and sea

*Culzean Castle with the Fair Coves
engraving by William Miller*

**By the 18th century, great changes were
coming to Ayrshire. Land use and agriculture
became more systematic, and the present day
field system enclosed the land.**

The Kennedys were at the forefront, and
set about improving their vast estates.

In 1744 Thomas, later 9th Earl of
Cassillis, inherited Culzean Castle. It was still

then a medieval structure, built for defence, and he set about improving it.

He eventually made it his home. In 1762 he inherited the earldom, and with it Cassillis Castle. However, he chose to remain at Culzean.

In 1775 his brother David became the 10th Earl, and made even more improvements. He called in Robert Adam, who transformed Culzean into what has been called the finest clifftop castle in Europe.

Gone were its fortifications, and in their place were elegant drawing rooms and staircases. A magnificent round saloon was built above the clifftops between 1785 and 1787, and this is probably the Castle's most famous feature.

The Earldom passed to Captain Archibald Kennedy, David's cousin. From that time, the Kennedys have always had a close connection with the sea.

After the 12th Earl, who was created Marquis of Ailsa in 1831, the line passed peacefully down to the present day.

The 2nd marquis, Archibald, established

a ship building yard at the foot of the cliffs beneath Culzean. The 3rd marquis, also called Archibald, put it on a commercial footing, eventually moving it to the village of Maidens near Turnberry and thence to Troon.

Thus was born the great Ailsa Shipbuilding Company, which still exists today, though the Kennedys no longer have an interest in it.

Culzean is now a National Trust for Scotland property, and is open to the public. The Kennedys once more live at Cassillis.

The most famous person to bear the name was John Fitzgerald Kennedy (1917-1963), President of the United States. He came from a Boston family whose Catholic forebears had emigrated from Ireland.

The Kennedys were once the premier family in south west Scotland, and an old rhyme sums up their great power:

> *Twixt Galloway and the toun of Air,*
> *Portpatrick and the cruives of Cree,*
> *No man needs think for there to bide,*
> *Unless he court with Kennedie.*

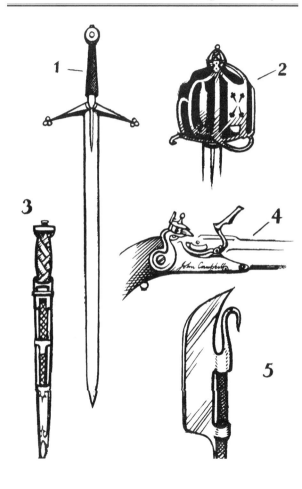

Highland weapons

1)   The claymore or two-handed sword
(fifteenth or early sixteenth century)

2)   Basket hilt of broadsword
made in Stirling, 1716

3)   Highland dirk
(eighteenth century)

4)   Steel pistol *(detail)* made in Doune

5)   Head of Lochaber Axe as carried
in the '45 and earlier